Going Back to School
During Coronavirus

story by
Rachel Saunders

illustrated by
Natalia Scabuso

Today is my first day back to school!

Last year school was cancelled because of a germ that was making people sick.

If the germ gets inside your body, you don't feel well.

Mom says we have to learn to protect ourselves. That means school will be a little different this year.

I remember when I got the flu. I couldn't play and I had to stay in bed for a long time. It was terrible!

I don't want my friends and family to get sick, so I'll do my part to stop this germ from spreading.

Staying safe from germs means I need some special school supplies.

A face mask to cover my mouth and nose, and hand sanitizer to clean my hands when I can't wash them.

Time for school!

I'm excited to see my friends and meet my new teacher!

But I'm nervous, too.
All these changes are a little scary.

In my classroom, I see that the desks are really far apart. The tape on the floor shows me where to walk.

I take my seat and wait for class to start.

My teacher, Mrs. Smith, shows us how to stop germs from spreading at school.

We need to learn how to do this so we don't get sick or bring the germs home.

Washing our hands is very important to keep germs away. So let's practice!

First, we wet our hands with warm water. Then, we lather them with soap and scrub for a long time. Mom taught me to sing "Happy Birthday" twice while I scrub!

When I am done singing, I rinse my hands with water and dry them.

If we aren't wearing a mask, we have to be extra careful. Mrs. Smith taught us never to cough or sneeze into the air. If we cough, we should cough into our elbow.

If we sneeze, we should use a tissue, and throw it in the trash. Then, wash our hands with soap and water.

It is also important to tell our teacher if we don't feel well. That way we don't get our friends or the teacher sick, too!

Soon, it's time for lunch. We make a line to walk to the cafeteria.

Space stops germs from jumping from one friend to another, so we leave space between ourselves as we walk. It's a really long line!

Lunchtime is my favorite time of day.

Some things have changed this year, though. We can't share our food like we used to. If you touch something and then give it to a friend, they could get sick.

So we have to keep our hands and things to ourselves.

One thing that hasn't changed is getting to talk and play with our friends.

We can't get super close together, but we can still play games like soccer.

We have to help remind our friends not to touch their face. I remind my friend, and he thanks me.

My friend and I love soccer!

My teacher is proud of me!

I am doing my best to keep everyone healthy.

School sure is different this year, but together, we can beat this germ!

It's time to go home.

I can't wait to share all the things I learned on my first day.

I'm so excited for school again tomorrow!